The Small Ta

Master The Unwritten Code of Social Skills and How Simple Training Can Help You Connect Effortlessly With Anyone. Little-Known Hacks to Talk to People with Self-Confidence

Written By

Daniel Fine

within this book has been derived from various sources. Please consult a licensed professional before attempting any techniques outlined in this book.

By reading this document, the reader agrees that under no circumstances is the author responsible for any losses, direct or indirect, which are incurred as a result of the use of information contained within this document, including, but not limited to, — errors, omissions, or inaccuracies.

Table of Contents

Introduction

No matter how seemingly "isolated" a person is, he or she needs other people. That is the bottom line. If you are reading this book, you are headed in the right direction, because instead of running away from the issue or saying that shyness is just "who you are," you are actually looking to solve your situation head on. I congratulate you. This book will help you become more social.

Your success depends on how much time, effort, and focus you put into it. Make no mistake about it: To benefit more fully from our social interaction and contribute more value to other people, we need to improve our social skills. This book guides you through a practical, success-focused approach to improving those skills.

Instead of rehashing and recycling the same old psychological stuff and jargon that you get from other social-skill–builder books, this book instead walks you through several steps you can take to gain quick results.

Please note: While this book will teach you how to improve your skills in getting along with others, you are not going to transform from a social outcast to a hero overnight.

I need you to get that idea out of your head. This book is

not one of those heavily hyped “magical” and social transformational ones. This book instead focuses on practical steps you can take on a day-to-day basis. Despite what you may have read from other books or the impressions you may have gained from them, overcoming shyness and becoming more social really takes effort. I know that is probably not the kind of message you want to hear, but it is the truth. It is the message that you need to hear.

Accordingly, you need to manage your expectations. The bottom line is, you get out what you put in. I don’t mean to put a damper on your expectations for this book, but I would rather set you up for the long, hard road ahead and condition you for ultimate success rather than let you down by hyping up quick results.

To reach the height of social mastery, you need to constantly practice, scale up, and optimize the information you will learn here. It is important to note that the information I am going to share with you is just the starting point. Feel free to slice and dice and mix and match the suggestions to fit your personality and your set of circumstances.

Still, just by implementing the information I provide you, you will be in a better position than you are now in terms of getting along with others and making a better impression.

Chapter 1: Addressing the Elephant in the Room: Fear

Shyness is not something shameful. Everyone feels shy sometimes. Do you remember the time when you had to stand in front of the whole class to introduce yourself? Or that time when you had to be in front of your boss and other business partners so that you could deliver your report? How about that moment when you had to give a speech at your best friend's wedding or on your parents' anniversary?

Even when you just meet people for the first time, it is not uncommon to have a feeling of uneasiness that keeps you from saying the right things or that makes you want to run far away as quickly as possible. You feel nervous and anxious, and all you can do is wish that you had not been put in that situation in the first place.

Many people have the misconception that only introverted people experience shyness. Introverts, after all, are known for avoiding social situations because they often prefer to be by themselves rather than with other people. But being introverted is very different from having feelings of shyness. On the contrary, shyness is that tendency to feel tense or awkward and sometimes even worried during social encounters. Most of the time, this feeling of unease is associated with social interactions with strangers, but it can also happen in different situations.

Shyness can be observed through certain symptoms. Some people who are shy blush easily when faced with an awkward moment. For others, shyness brings with it sweating, the quick pounding of the heart, and even the feeling of an upset stomach. There are also times when shyness creates mental manifestations such as shy people having negative feelings about themselves. People who are shy tend to worry about how other people view them, and thus, they would rather withdraw from social interactions than worry about other people's perceptions of them.

Everyone feels shy at least once in their lives. Even the most confident person may feel shy about meeting the person of his or her dreams and even more so when meeting that person's parents and other family members. A well-established businessman may also feel anxious when dealing with new partners or perhaps when addressing the shareholders despite the fact that he or she is already very much respected and admired. And even the world's greatest leaders may stumble and falter when given unexpected praises or comments.

Again, there is nothing to be ashamed of when it comes to being shy. It is natural, just as breathing is natural.

However, if you find yourself feeling shy and you know that the shyness is keeping you from doing what you must, then there is something that has to be done. Fortunately, there are more ways of overcoming shyness than you may think.

Feelings of shyness often come from being too self-conscious or from being overly worried about what other people think. In some cases, these feelings can lead to awkward social moments where the shy person stutters or finds it hard to maintain eye contact or any other level of physical contact. In the worst case, it can also lead to intense social phobia. The most common occurrences of shyness are associated with interactions with authority figures (such as teachers, bosses, and leaders), with romantic interests, and in various group settings.

Overcoming Shyness

Those who wish to overcome their shyness should put utmost importance into having a clear understanding about what their personal shyness is about.

Each person experiences shyness in a unique way. The cause for shyness varies between people, as do the signs and symptoms and the source or the reason for the shyness. Before you try to overcome your shyness, you should have a deeper understanding of what it is and from where it stems. By knowing the source, you have a much better chance of addressing the issue from its root and getting more favorable results.

There are three main reasons why people feel shy. First is a result of a weak self-image. When you see yourself as someone who is never good enough or someone who always acts the wrong way, chances are that you will be anxious around other people. Unfortunately, how you think about yourself or what you see yourself doing is often manifested into the real world. Therefore, if you believe that you will do something wrong, you probably will.

However, the solution is very simple—stop thinking so negatively about yourself! This advice is easier said than done, but it is one of the most fundamental ways of how you can overcome shyness. Remember that a weak self-image is just a voice inside your head. But that voice is your mind and what you are thinking. Tell that voice to shut up, or better yet, make that voice say something positive.

The second main reason why people tend to feel shy is that they are too conscious of how they appear to other people. It is only natural for human beings to be conscious about what other people may be thinking, but to be unable to function properly as a result is never good. Those who are shy because of this reason will spend hours preparing themselves so that they look presentable in front of other people.

Even so, they will always be conscious about every move they make and whether or not they are turning off others. The solution is to not focus on one's self too much. Other people are most likely thinking of things besides you, so you should do the same.

Finally, people tend to become shy because they have been labeled as such. When you are considered shy, there is a greater tendency to experience shyness in social situations. Even if you are willing to overcome the label, the problem is that those who have labeled you may still treat you as such. Then again, it is all just a matter of perception. So what if other people think you are shy? The more that others think this way, the greater the reason you have for proving them otherwise.

Each of these reasons has their own validity, but the simple fact is that you must get over these thoughts if you want to overcome shyness. Stop thinking negatively about yourself, do not stress yourself too much about what other people may think, and get over what other people do think about you. Overcoming shyness starts with accepting that you are shy, understanding why that is so, and making a conscious effort to turn things around.

Identifying Other Obstacles You May Have to Overcome During Small Talk

Anxiety

Anxiety about social settings and being around strangers causes nervousness, fear, and apprehension. This condition makes people view the situation as threatening, worry about what people are thinking of them, and question others' intentions when they approach or make a compliment, etc.

There may even be some physical symptoms such as increased heart rate, sweating, and breathing changes.

First, understand you are not alone. Social anxiety afflicts millions of people on all levels in all walks of life, but it does not mean that you have a mental illness, nor is it indicative that you need clinical help. There are common ways to adjust and overcome normal anxiety.

One way is simple acceptance. We already understand from the onset that first meetings are going to be awkward. The main rule is to lower your expectations of yourself and stop trying to be perfect. It is all right to be human and make a mistake or say something that you might think was stupid. So what if it was? Then you get an honest laugh, which is always a great icebreaker—you just burst the door wide open and became approachable.

Another effective way to battle social anxiety is to prepare a discussion topic prelist, which is very empowering and builds confidence. A prelist for small talk would include subjects such as a few preselected noncontroversial current news topics, hot viral video topics, new smartphone apps, movies, books, restaurants, travel, or anything of a nature that is commonly inclusive but noncontroversial or argumentative.

A preselected topic list will allow you to focus on interaction as opposed to introduction. The suggested subjects are chosen to help you block the worry of what people may think because they are neutral and do not release personal information about you.

With that thought in mind, armor yourself with a beaming smile, relax your shoulders, take a couple of deep breaths, then start looking for a few familiar faces. After you have made some familiar contacts and have gotten your footing under you, then start working the room. Very importantly in this situation, do not worry so much about what people think of you. In these types of settings, the base truth is that most of them don’t remember half of what they said, what you said, or what others said because they are battling themselves the same way you are.

Body Language

To appear open and be perceived as receptive requires being mindful of your body language. Keeping open body language maintains and projects a friendly appearance. To accomplish said openness that does not get confused as tawdry or flirting, start out simply with a whole-face smile that is delivered with a relaxed face and touches the eyes. Make sure not to come across as having the rictus grin of Botox or lascivious by practicing in a mirror in your spare time. Also, keep your face in the direction of the person with whom you are conversing.

Keep your arms and legs uncrossed, but especially your arms, at all times. The uncrossed legs require a little more thought; if you are standing, your uncrossed legs should be no more than shoulder width in foot separation. When sitting, for females, crossed ankles and tucked feet are perfectly acceptable but not required; just make sure to keep your knees together. This tidbit is what differentiates between appearing flirty and appearing open.

At all times, keep your hands open and palms facing outward. This gesture projects openness and approachability. Occasionally reaching out and touching someone's arm or hand during conversation is also perfectly acceptable. You may also want to loosen your tie or remove a jacket as another sign of open approachability.

The behaviors you always want to avoid are nuisance movements, such as leg shaking, leg swinging, hair twisting, finger tapping, scratching, or repeatedly checking your watch. And by all means, put the cell phone away.

Minding your body language is another form of mental distraction that will help you overcome your social anxiety issues and, in due time, will become second nature without thought.

Diffusing Social Gaming

In every diverse gathering of people, there always have been and always will be those few who seem to go overboard to sabotage the event. There are effective and classic ways to diffuse these situations.

There are always the argumentative ones who just look for confrontation in everything that is being said. A way of dealing with them is to simply respond to their remarks with polite dismissal. You can excuse yourself politely and then move on about the room, maintaining your own personal dignity by never engaging them.

It seems like there is always a hanger-on type at every gathering who follows you around, shadowing your every move. You can simply have pity on them and realize their inadequacies in their current environment, or you can use the escape method by ducking into the restroom for a few minutes or introducing them to someone else—especially a known talker—giving a quick exit explanation and then moving on. This tactic will be effective but will not be perceived as rude or mean. The person you ditched will most likely interpret it as you being gracious.

The next problem personality type is the one you cannot get to let you go. We have all met that person who just goes on and on talking about the same thing. In this instance, you may momentarily break eye contact only long enough to quickly scan the room for a familiar face and a reason to escape. Or you and a friend may have a preset escape plan; then by all means, give the SOS. Just remember to retain those good manners and end the conversation or excuse yourself before exiting the person's company.

There will be other uncomfortable situations that you will encounter, but many of these methods should be an effective response to maintain your dignity in any and all those types of situations.

Chapter 2: The Powerful End Goal of Being Good with People: Confidence

Conversational Confidence Is Key

Confidence is crucial for every conversationalist. It will be difficult without it to convince people to believe in you when you do not believe in yourself. Even if you have every strategy for success at your disposal, if you don't have the confidence to back it up, it is going to be all for nothing.

Why Is Confidence So Important?

Here is what happens when you lack the confidence to pull off small talk (or anything else for that matter, not just social interaction):

1. Fear Will Always Be What Holds You Back

If you are regularly ruled by fear of and anxiety over everything that could go wrong, there will be many things that you don't do or try. You will become so afraid of failing that you will fail to do anything at all, even if it is something that would benefit you in the long run. Something as simple as walking up to someone and saying "Hello, how are you?"

can be challenging to manage since you are so afraid of being embarrassed.

2. You Are Going to Miss Out on Opportunities

Especially at work, small talk is a potential networking opportunity that could lead to bigger and better things for your career. Missing out and letting them pass you by is linked closely with the point above; that same fear is going to stop you and make you hesitant about grabbing opportunities right in front of you. In life, it could prevent you from forging new friendships, relationships, and more.

3. You Will Find It Hard to be Happy

People who lack confidence generally have feelings of low self-esteem. They are always thinking about their flaws, which makes it hard for them to be happy. When you focus on your inadequacies, how are you going to concentrate on everything you are supposed to do to be better? Negativity is a powerful emotion, one that comes much more easily than positivity.

How to Become a More Confident Person

Confidence is vital, especially when making an impression on someone during small talk. Being confident gives you the courage to know that you can manage the situation you are in and that you can control how a conversation is going.

1. Mind over Matter

Confidence begins in your mind, and it is a state of mind that you and only you have the power to change. You must want to change the way you think about yourself and let go of negative connotations. There are plenty of ways you can help strengthen your mind-set over time. Tell yourself that you are a confident person who is more than capable of handling anything that comes your way. For instance, meditation is a good exercise for the mind, body, and soul. You can also try recording affirmations; write them down on Post-it Notes and stick them in places where you can easily see them so you are continually surrounded by messages of positive reinforcement. Again, it is about what works best for you. Try to start strengthening your mind to think more positively.

2. Identify What You Need to Work On

Self-doubt is one of the most significant mental obstacles to overcome when it comes to building confidence in yourself. You have probably been saddled with self-doubt for a long time, and it can seem impossible to think in any other way. It will be a struggle at first, but it must be done if you want to begin developing and transforming into a better version of yourself. Begin by making a list of what you think are the areas you need to work on. Once you are done, make a list of possible suggestions about what you can do to improve those areas. It does not necessarily have to be massive, drastic changes all at once. It won't do you any good if you are feeling overwhelmed. Start small and record achievable goals that you can accomplish and then repeat the process once you start completing them.

3. Acknowledge What You Have Done Well

Did you handle something particularly well today? Even better than you thought? It is time to start acknowledging it. Make it a habit from today onward to recognize and congratulate yourself on a job well done each time you have made an accomplishment. After all, it is an achievement, and every achievement deserves recognition. For example, if you had a particularly successful small-talk session today, fantastic work! Great job. You should be proud of your accomplishments, which also helps build your confidence over time.

4. Make a List of Your Strengths

Sometimes it is easier to believe something when you see it written down in front of you. If you are having trouble making a list of your pros, enlist the help of family and friends. Ask them to tell you what they admire the most about you and what they think you are good at doing. Ask them to help you identify your strengths. It can help boost your confidence knowing how other people think about you; they may list attributes that you did not even recognize in yourself. Once you have compiled your list, go through it daily until you firmly believe in each point and you feel an increase in your confidence level.

5. You Need to Look Good to Feel Good

The way you look and feel about yourself is going to make a difference in your confidence levels. How much time do you spend taking care of your appearance and the way you present yourself? Is your hair fixed neatly? Do you wear clothes that fit well? The way you look is going to be the first thing that people notice about you when you introduce yourself and taking some time to look and feel your best will help. You don't have to buy a new wardrobe to look the part, just work with what you have right now. Make sure your clothes always look clean, are comfortable, and make you feel good.

Chapter 3: The Secret Advantage to Knowing the Social Skills Code and the Human Mind

Tips and Tricks before Small Talk

Interactions, in general, are very simple in nature, although complex individually. Every interaction is based on a certain motive that can be expressed through interest.

If a person finds you interesting or if you have something of value that can be acquired through social interaction, then social interaction will be easy to achieve.

These statements lead us to the conclusion that you must possess certain value to be a person of interest, someone worthy of social interaction.

Thus, the goal of this book: to explain how to engage in small talk with people and use this skill to your advantage to accomplish your goals. Since small talk is a form of communication that can be considered a social interaction, then it is very valuable to understand what your ultimate goal should be "underneath the curtains."

People feel badly when they are rejected or feel unwelcome somewhere or in some situations. It is a natural feeling, but these situations tend to scare people and lead them to the circle of blame that results in even more rejections and social failures.

You should never blame someone else for bad things that happen to you in social interactions.

Instead, the first question to ask yourself should be, “What could I have done better in that situation to avoid this unwanted outcome?” Objective reflection on your actions is the best way to achieve your goals in the long run.

The cruel reality of life is that we cannot expect to be accepted simply because we exist. It is true that we have feelings and rejections that make us feel badly, but in order to be accepted anywhere and by anyone, you need to prove your worth and value in some way.

A simple example can be derived from a situation where a man approaches a woman with the intention of seducing her, getting her number, or asking her out on a date.

To achieve his goal, this man is expected to impress the woman in some way and create attraction and interest between them.

If he fails, the only person he should blame is himself, and bitterness is not the solution. He cannot expect to approach the woman, startle her, ask for her number in the first sentence, and expect a positive outcome.

This is an unrealistic view of this situation, and it needs to be corrected. You must present a certain value and need to do it successfully to expect a positive outcome in any social interaction. One of the main goals of this guide is to provide you with some tools that can help you present yourself as a person of value, making you someone worth the time and effort to talk to and interact with positively.

Read a Book

Why do people read books, and why should you read them according to your goal to be a better engager? Some people simply enjoy the way information is formatted in the books.

Anything used to distribute information has its own distinctive format, just like books have their own form and rules that should be followed when writing them.

Most books are not limited by a certain number of pages, which means that content can be written about in detail, enabling the reader to achieve a greater understanding of the subject at hand in comparison to other media used to provide information, such as movies.

So how can reading a book help you be better at small talk?

What value do you get from this action? The easiest way to start or continue a conversation with someone is to have things in common with them. Similar interests can lead to a rich discussion about the given topic. The main problem is choosing what to read and how to invest your time in reading it. (You can always find some time to read a book because it is something you can take with you. Perhaps you can read it while on public transportation or in waiting rooms, during breaks, etc.)

Depending on your goals, you should choose the topic. If you know someone who reads books and you want to have better small talk with that person, ask them what topics they like and read books based on similar subjects.

You do not really have to like the content; just have an opinion on it, and do not be afraid to share your opinion. Respect the opinion of the other person, and have a nice discussion about the content you have read.

Watch a Movie or a Popular Television Series

The art of small talk consists of an ability to find easy topics of relatable conversation. These topics need to be something that people feel comfortable discussing and something they feel a need to share their opinion about.

Movies and television have become a big part of people's

lives since they were first introduced into society. The magic that happens on the screen has never stopped amazing people all around the world, and because of that, people who bring that magic into our lives have risen as stars, becoming icons of wealth, beauty, and talent. By watching movies, TV shows, etc., we subconsciously observe how other people act. And we can choose to mimic their actions.

Their value is indisputable, and there is something in that concept we can take and learn from. They have demonstrated their value with their talent on the screen, and we watch that as a form of art because we choose to do so.

This principle can be applied to small talk, where we demonstrate our value through our knowledge of the topics we choose to talk about, as well as the charisma and energy we show when presenting those topics, and in the end, we are judged and evaluated by those who share the conversation with us.

Some people have a natural predisposition for animated conversation, and it is easy for them to be "chatty" and to be wanted as company.

If you do not think you are that kind of person, you should not worry because anything can be learned, and small talk is just another skill to acquire.

There is a huge population of people that follows their stars as icons in their lives, imagining they could someday meet them or be like them. Or perhaps they just enjoy the work these people do. This fandom is a great potential for starting a conversation because people are highly motivated to share their opinions on matters they are passionate about. Getting together to watch a movie or a television show can also be an excellent social activity.

Enroll in a Class

The extension of the strategy about increasing your value as a conversational partner centers around the variety of topics you can talk about.

Aside from usual topics such as global events, movies, television, and books, you should show people there is a deeper side of you that seeks knowledge within the classroom. The best knowledge you can acquire to increase your worth as a person to talk to is the knowledge of speaking foreign languages.

This ability is highly rewarded and admired among people all around the world, and it is always convenient, especially if you like to travel to foreign countries.

This skill is especially effective when trying to impress

potential dates or business associates. Imagine a very possible situation, like meeting an attractive singleton. When meeting new people, you usually want to keep it simple and not personal, so small talk is in order.

A couple of compliments in French would likely increase attraction because you would appear capable of learning several languages as well as demonstrate that you are someone with a wide range of interests, instantly making you interesting.

Finding an opportunity and excuse to speak in a foreign language is a powerful demonstration of value. But if you wish to compliment someone in a foreign language, you should follow up with a translation and explanation. However, you must be careful not to brag or speak too long in the foreign language, because if there is no one who understands you, people could start feeling uncomfortable.

Learning a new language shows you are an intriguing person, but it must be done wisely and subtly. There are lots of ways to enrich your skill set by going to extra classes. You do not need much time: usually two or three hours a week will be enough for you to be able to speak comfortably in a year or two.

Not all changes need be fast or costly. There are lots of free classes available, and there are plenty of interesting subjects to learn about.

Find a New Hobby

The need for variety in your life continues. The more you know, the more confident you will feel about your conversation potential. An important aspect about small talk is that not all people want to hear about everything. Certain people are interested in certain topics. You cannot affect that, and it is not wise to try to force someone to like something new during small talk.

The best thing for you to do is to make sure you are well equipped with knowledge of different subjects so you can accommodate various conversation partners. Finding out what people like to talk about is an important step to take while making conversation.

It is not that hard to find out what people are interested in because the solution is very simple. Just ask. If you simply ask someone about their interests, there is no reason why that person will not share some information about themselves if they are ready and willing to socialize.

Once you are involved in the conversation, you may have the opportunity to discuss your own interests. Be prepared to talk about your job, family, and hobbies. If you don’t have any hobbies, start one. What hobby you choose is completely up to you, but it is important for it to be something constructive that you genuinely enjoy. You may even wish to pick up the same hobby as someone with whom you have an interest.

Prepare Various Jokes

Being a funny person makes you wanted company. We all like that person who brings joy when they arrive.

Humor is tricky, and it varies from person to person. Knowing how to make someone laugh is a great way to get on their good side, and it is a great way to spend time together.

The best small talk is filled with laughter on both sides. Those conversations stick to you like little boosts of energy, helping you go through the day despite all the difficulties you may encounter.

This "vibe" follows your future encounters as well. Every time you see the person with whom you had good laughs, new laughs are a lot easier to make.

It is a bit different when you want to become the person who brings laughs to the table. It is definitely something that can be practiced, but it takes a lot of effort and courage.

This effort and courage consists of that "try, fail, and learn" method, where you must try the joke, risk failing, and if you fail, learn from that and change what needs changing in the future.

The best solution is to prepare jokes that are somewhat popular or come from good professional comedians so you minimize the chances of failure. But that is only ten percent of the work because telling a good joke is all about the way you present the material.

When telling a joke, you need to have good timing. Dramatic pauses are very important as are facial expressions, your vocals, and gestures.

Telling jokes can almost be considered an art form because it is not easy to do at all. You can probably practice with people you already know and feel safe with before trying to tell jokes to strangers. Your goal is to make good small talk, and this is a powerful tool to know.

If you are not good at telling jokes, maybe you can try your luck with narrating. Hearing stories can be just as fun for the audience—try telling scary stories in a fitting environment or inspirational stories for people who need them. Stories are easier to tell, but they need to be adapted to the audience.

Some people are not patient enough to listen to a long story, or they are not always capable of understanding its content if it is too metaphorical. Take these facts into consideration when preparing material for conversation.

Invest in Accessories

Making yourself visible can help you achieve your goals and put you out there to be noticed. Having gadgets or accessories on your body can help you with approaches.

If you have trouble breaking the ice, one solution is to let someone else break it for you. Just make yourself visible and accessible, and the situation will play itself out.

A good outfit, bracelets, rings, necklaces, etc. will make you more visible to people and make it easier for them to break the ice. For example, it is very easy to approach someone who has a tattoo and say, "Hey, what a nice tattoo. What does it mean?" This comment will hopefully start a nice chat.

Accessories that hold meaning to you are your best option because if someone is interested in the trinket you are wearing and asks where you got it, you always have an interesting story about the time you went on a trip and got a necklace or that time your friends had the bracelet made for you. Telling the story of how you acquired the trinket will easily carry a conversation instead of destroying it by saying, "It is just a trinket I bought at the mall."

This type of response sends out negative energy because it halts a conversation that could have been very successful if you had just told a small story about yourself. A negative response may make a listener change the topic of the conversation, and that is somewhat unnatural. The best conversations are when topics come naturally.

What Not to Do

Like most forms of discourse, small talk carries with it a set of taboos. Those engaged in small talk will want to navigate around certain topics, refrain from asking too many unrelated questions, avoid giving inappropriate or offensive compliments, prevent themselves from name-dropping, and avoid pitching products to conversation partners.

Topics to Avoid

Small talk includes some topics that communicators should avoid in most situations, like religion and politics. People tend to have strong opinions about these topics. Additionally, these subjects lend themselves to a highly subjective nature. Communicators who bring religion and politics into small talk risk getting themselves into an intense argument, especially when both parties have strong, opposing opinions.

In very specific circumstances, religion and politics serve as appropriate topics of small talk. For example, a churchgoer may find herself engaged in pleasant small talk regarding religion with the woman next to her in the pew. The two communicators in this situation likely have similar views regarding religion. In this particular case, the two may bond over the topic. However, in most situations, religion, like politics, acts as a taboo topic that communicators should avoid in the context of small talk.

Furthermore, individuals should avoid bringing up death during small talk. Death, as a topic, may conjure up unpleasant memories and experiences in your conversation partner. Plus, different cultures have widely varying beliefs and customs regarding death, so a focus on death makes it unlikely that strangers will connect as they discuss it from different perspectives.

Third, avoid talking about sex. Small talk does not make an appropriate medium for the discussion of sex. Much like with death, different cultures celebrate and understand sex in a variety of ways. Discussing sex often makes strangers feel uncomfortable, especially when the two understand sex in very different ways.

Next, small talk should exclude past relationships. The

thought of past relationships often brings up unpleasant memories or negative emotions, such as regret, heartbreak, anger, and sadness. People on a first date should take extreme care to avoid the topic of past relationships. In addition to bringing up bad memories, talking about past relationships on a first date hints that one still cares enough about their exes to warrant bringing them up to an unfamiliar acquaintance. Additionally, dating should establish the possibility of a future together, not a look back on the past. Save discussing exes for a future deeper conversation.

Fifth, conversers want to avoid bringing up people's personal affairs. Many people believe that personal affairs are a private matter and are therefore inappropriate for small talk. You may hear a rumor that your coworker's wife filed for divorce, but unless you know your coworker very well, you should avoid asking them or anyone else about it. However, if your coworker brings up their divorce in conversation, you may ask them about it if both of you are willing to discuss it further. In most cases, keep quiet about personal affairs. Personal affairs include topics like health, romantic relationships, family relationships, mental status, and financial situations. At this moment, think of two of your personal affairs that you would not want your acquaintances to talk about, and now you may understand why it is not appropriate to bring up personal affairs during small talk.

Finally, and building upon a point mentioned above, communicators should avoid bringing up personal finance during small talk. Small talk can include impersonal finance topics, such as the stock market, the economy, and a description of one's career or profession. However, individuals engaged in small talk should avoid inquiring into the other person's salary/wage/earnings or net worth. Do not ask someone how much they get paid. Additionally, many people consider it inappropriate for strangers to reveal their own income level.

Politics, religion, death, sex, past relationships, personal affairs, and personal finance may serve as appropriate topics in very specific circumstances. In general, however, individuals should avoid discussing these topics with strangers and acquaintances during small talk.

Unrelenting Questioning

Small talk involves reciprocating discourse between conversational partners. As such, certain behaviors find themselves inappropriate for small talk. One such behavior involves constructing a conversation out of nothing but questions.

Avoid asking question after question. Nonstop questioning may have its place in certain situations, such as interrogation rooms, courtroom trials, and job interviews. However, repeatedly questioning a conversation partner does not function well for small talk. Consider how you would feel if, during a casual conversation, somebody asked you a question, you answered it, and then you received more unrelated questions in return. Many people feel interrogated in this type of situation. Repeated questioning gives off the impression that the questioner has more interest in getting their conversation partner to say things than getting to know their conversation partner. Keep follow-up questions relevant to the topic at hand.

The Wrong Kind of Compliments

Compliments make a wonderful tactic for improving small talk. However, if used incorrectly, compliments can have an adverse effect on conversations and interpersonal relationships as a whole. It is especially important to avoid giving inappropriate compliments during small talk, which often sets the tone for the rest of the interaction. Compliments can go wrong in a number of ways. Avoid complimenting too regularly, complimenting the wrong traits, and giving compliments in front of the wrong people.

First, avoid complimenting too much. By giving out

numerous compliments, you assign less meaning to each compliment. Consider that if you give out one compliment, you recognize another person's admirable trait, whatever that may be. If you give someone a hundred compliments, they do not carry much weight individually. The other person will just see you as someone who gives out compliments rather than someone with an eye for their outstanding traits. Keep compliments meaningful by only giving them out when you have a good reason to do so.

Next, conversers will want to avoid making compliments that praise incorrect traits. Experts recommend avoiding compliments that revolve around the body parts of others. You will also want to make sure that the compliments you give relate to the situation at hand. For example, if your coworker just gave a strong presentation in front of a group, you would be better off complimenting their public speaking skills rather than their shoes.

Another thing to keep in mind is that when giving compliments, avoid giving them in front of the wrong people. For example, imagine you are out on a date at a restaurant. Assume that on the previous night, you praised your date for her ability to cook fried rice. Avoid telling the restaurant's chef that he makes the best fried rice you ever had while your date is present. If you make this compliment, your date night may not go exactly as you would have liked.

Name-Dropping

Name-dropping will not make you more likable, cooler, or more popular. In fact, it often has the opposite effect. People who name-drop frequently demonstrate that they do not perceive themselves as competent. Instead, they rely on associations with people more famous than themselves to bolster their image.

Imagine you are talking to an acquaintance about an upcoming project at work, and they repeatedly mention that they personally know the actor and fifteen-time WWE world champion, John Cena. The conversation might play out like this:

You: “So I was looking at what I have on the horizon at work, and next week, the boss wants to have a meeting about proper attire. I mean, I understand, but I don’t think it’s necessary. Nobody in the office really dresses that outlandishly.”

Acquaintance: “Hmmm . . . well, when I met John Cena, he told me that his bosses enforce a strict dress code at live events. It could just be a push for increased professionalism.”

You: “True, it just seems weird for our company. What do

you think about company dress codes?"

Acquaintance: "Well, I don't think people should be forced to fit in. In fact, my friend John Cena used to get a lot of flak for wrestling in denim shorts, but his attire helped him stand out and become the star he is today."

In this case, the acquaintance mentions his association with a celebrity every chance he gets. This name-dropping conveys that the acquaintance feels inadequate on his own. He hopes that his connection with higher-status individuals will demonstrate that the higher-status people have endorsed him as an acquaintance. Most people will see through name-dropping and assume that the name-dropper feels the need to constantly remind others about their connections to celebrities. You do not need to mention such connections to establish your status. Avoid name-dropping.

The Salesperson

Have you ever answered your front door to a salesperson asking you to buy something? Many door-to-door sales companies train their employees to make a few seconds of small talk with potential customers before pitching the product. If your goal involves genuinely connecting with others, do not try to sell them something or solicit donations. Making a sales pitch can cause them to wonder if you only wanted to get to know them so that they would buy your product. You may be involved with a great fundraiser or charity, but most people would feel obligated to buy something from a friendly acquaintance. This feeling of obligation can put them in an uncomfortable position. You do not want to be the person who makes others feel uncomfortable. If you must ask for money, skip the small talk and make your intentions known up front.

Chapter 4: What to Say After "Hello"

Before small talk begins, there are steps you can take to prepare for it. Preparation may make the difference between a stimulating, low-risk conversation and an awkward exchange of words. To prepare for small talk, minimize distractions and reduce anxiety.

Minimizing distractions increases the likelihood of engaging in small talk. Put away electronic devices, including cell phones. Do not wear headphones. When at home, turn off the television and computer screens. By minimizing distractions, conversers are more likely to notice one another's conversational cues.

Next, the thought of starting conversations with unfamiliar people can cause individuals to feel anxious. According to psychologist Dr. Thomas A. Richards, social anxiety is one of the top three most common mental problems in the United States. Small talkers should take steps to lower their anxiety levels.

Constantly keep reminding yourself that your prospective conversation partner has uncertainties too. Remember that the uncertainty reduction theory suggests that people gather information through discourse that helps them reduce uncertainties about one another. Initiating small talk may seem daunting at first, but as the conversation flows, both parties to small talk become more familiar with each other and thus more relaxed. Additionally, consider that small talk, by nature, is a low-risk activity.

To further reduce anxiety, psychologists recommend a combination of breathing and visualization exercises. Take a deep breath, hold it for a few seconds, and exhale. Focus on the sensations of the breath coming in and out of your nose. Humboldt State University psychologist Brian A. McElwain advocates for this breathing practice, often integrating it into the Mindfulness meditation group that he facilitates. By focusing on the breath, individuals take their focus away from the distracting nervous chatter in their heads.

Psychologists also recommend visualization exercises. Psychotherapist Dr. Cathryne Maciolek suggests that people can use visualization exercises to cope with anxiety and better operate throughout the day. Imagine yourself having a fun, low-risk conversation with your prospective conversation partner. Research shows that if you can imagine yourself doing something, you are more likely to do that thing successfully.

The real world moves quickly, but taking a few seconds to

engage in practices like breathing and visualization can make a significant and noticeable difference in anxiety levels. With the right frame of mind, you can make small talk much easier on yourself.

Initiating Small Talk

Many conversations begin with small talk. Small talk provides parties to a conversation with a relatively safe form of discourse. Think of small talk like the "feeling out" portion of the conversation. Initiating small talk consists of three phases: locating and establishing a shared experience, revealing information relating to that shared experience, and finally, asking a related question. Communication scholar Dr. Carol Fleming refers to these steps as anchoring, revealing, and encouraging.

To initiate small talk, you should first identify an experience that you share with your potential conversation partner. Classmates share the same teacher. Strangers walking down the same street share the weather. A concert's audience members share the experience of attending the concert. The next time you find yourself in a room with at least a couple of other people, try to identify three interesting experiences that you share with everyone else present. Your setting probably contains a myriad of experiences that you share.

Once this shared experience is identified, make a comment or remark about it. For example, assume that a professor has just given a stimulating lecture to his class. A student in this class named Brett might say to his classmate Amanda, “Professor Gus is so smart.” At this point, Brett has identified and established a shared experience that he has with Amanda: the professor.

Assuming that Amanda responds favorably, Brett should continue into the conversation by sharing information about himself that relates to the professor. He might add, “I feel like I miss out whenever I don’t attend his class.” Here, Brett reveals something about himself. By relating himself to the shared experience, Brett gives Amanda material to which she can relate.

Finally, Brett should ask an open-ended question relating to the professor. He could ask, “How do you feel about the upcoming test?” This question encourages Amanda to pick up the conversation. Brett should listen to her answer attentively. At this point, Brett has successfully initiated small talk with a classmate.

Communicators initiate small talk by identifying and remarking on a shared experience, sharing related information about themselves, and asking an open-ended, relevant question. Anchor yourself and your conversation partner to the same reality, reveal something about yourself, and encourage your conversation partner to contribute. Dr. Fleming teaches these steps using the acronym ARE: anchor, reveal, encourage.

Once initiated, small talk can go in an infinite number of directions. Part of small talk's fun involves its unpredictability. As such, it would not be possible to provide readers with word-for-word scripts that guarantee a successful small talk. In fact, memorized scripts will likely prevent conversers from fully engaging others as they try to remember the right words to say.

How to Ask Excellent Questions

Aside from being a great way to explore further topics, open-ended questions are great conversation starters, particularly straight after your initial statement and introducing yourself. Avoid the yes-or-no questions that can cut the conversation short if the person doesn't have much to say themselves. There are ways you can turn even the most basic questions into open-ended questions. For example, rather than asking whether the person is having a good day, ask what they have been up to. This type of question allows the person to go through their day and also feels as though you are showing more interest in their day rather than just making generic conversation.

Similarly, instead of asking "Do you like this place, or do you come here often?" you can ask "What keeps you coming back?" This question keeps the conversation open and allows you to explore further topics rather than continually asking questions to keep the conversation moving, which can become frustrating. Keep variety in your discussion as it will keep the interaction interesting.

The Power of Listening

When you are in a conversation, it is just as important to make the other person feel as though you are listening as it is to be actively engaged in whatever it is they are saying. It is important to make an effort to listen with all your senses and make it clear to the other person that you really comprehend whatever it is they are talking about.

The following are physical signs of listening:

1. Smile

Smiling at the right times while you are listening says that you appreciate what the other person is saying or you agree broadly with the topic being discussed or the specific information being conveyed. When added to a simple head nod, a smile is a way to say that you understand what is being asked of you and you will go ahead and do it.

2. Eye Contact

Depending on how many people you are speaking to and what else is going on around the conversation, making eye contact is a great way for the other party to know that you are listening to what they are saying. Ensure you maintain enough eye contact to show you are interested, but do not keep doing it so intently that it is seen as inappropriate.

3. Posture

The posture you use while listening can say a lot about your thoughts on the information in the conversation being conveyed. If you are actively listening, you will want to make a point of leaning toward the person who is speaking. You will want to add to this by either resting your head on your hand while looking at the speaker or tilting your head to the side slightly to indicate you are listening.

4. Mirroring

Mirroring the actions and mannerisms of the person you are listening to is a subconscious way of letting them know that you both are on the same page. Mirroring should look natural, however, as being noticed trying to mimic certain expressions will make it appear that you are not listening at all. Alternatively, if you start mimicking the other person and then start doing your own gestures or expressions and see them mimic you, you will know you have control of the conversation.

5. Don't Appear Distracted

Even if you are listening intently, doing things like looking at your phone, fidgeting, or nitpicking your appearance will all give the speaker the assumption of the opposite. Give the person you are listening to your full attention, and they will assume you are listening more competently as a result.

6. Remember Key Points

If you want to show the other person that you were really listening, one of the best ways to do so is to remember key pieces of information about a conversation you had previously. Don't worry about remembering the details. The gist of the conversation will be enough to cause them to react favorably to your effort.

7. Ask Questions

While many people who feel awkward in conversation may believe that asking questions is a good way to imply you weren't paying attention; in reality, it is a great way to show you value what the other person is saying so much that you want to ensure you get it right. The questions you are asking should appear as though they are digging deeper on the topic, not simply rehashing what has already been said.

8. Clarification

Much like with asking questions, asking for clarification on what has been said, assuming the details have not already been clarified, is a great way to make it clear to the other person that you are definitely invested in what they have to say. It is important to ask for clarification all at once, however, as breaking it up can cause the conversation to feel stilted and unnatural.

Chapter 5: What a Good Conversation Looks Like and How to Start Gaining Confidence

Goals of Conversation and Small Talk

For some of us out there, speaking to someone in a casual atmosphere may be easy while speaking to someone in a more forced social situation may make us inclined to hide from the world. There are also instances where we fumble over our words, overact, fidget too much, say inappropriate things, or feel we need to fill the silence by saying something. Or perhaps it is as simple as being shy or having social anxieties. Learning the basics of communication is only part of your journey to improve your social skills. The other parts are for you to understand what your goals are and for you to actually put them into play.

There are three basic communication areas: nonverbal communication, basic social skills, and real-world application. Nonverbal communication normally deals with body language, which accounts for fifty-five percent of effective communication, while the verbal aspect accounts for the other forty-five percent and splits them into separate categories: the tone of voice and words. Your tone of voice accounts for thirty-eight percent of effective communication, while the words you and others say are the lowest at only seven percent. Now, why do you think that is? Why do you think we pick up on someone's body language and the sound of their voice more than what they are actually saying?

It is because unspoken forms of communication are universal. They are the first things we come to understand at a very young age. When a baby laughs, it must mean it thinks something is funny. When a baby cries, we instinctively think something is wrong. When we speak lovingly to a baby, they begin to respond not only to the voice but to the action that follows. In short, you can say it has been programmed into us since a very young age. It is something we have taught ourselves to recognize comfort, safety, and nourishment. As this is the very first thing we learned, we unknowingly take any indication of that safety and comfort from the people around us as we get older. We see gestures before we speak. We hear the tone before we listen to words. We understand the other person's message before we get involved with the conversation. Just by visually assessing someone and by understanding their tone, you get a notion of how the person may feel.

In addition to nonverbal aspects of communication, there

is listening, as stated earlier. Listening is actually a form of communication; however, we'll be focusing on active listening. This art of communication requires the listener to be engaged in the conversation by listening intently rather than trying to fill in the silence with words. This aspect of communication is very important to those who are trying to connect. They want someone who is going to listen and understand their message. If you are the quiet type already, then you are most likely already there, not because you are silent, but because you know how to listen and observe overall. Staying silent can work to your advantage at times when used properly.

In order to help you build a genuine rapport with others, active listening gives you the advantage of understanding your partner or group members more easily. This understanding opens up opportunities to chime in with some nuggets of wisdom after they are done speaking. Active listening demonstrates to others that you are willing to listen to what they have to say without judgment and help if need be. Thus, you are building trust between the two of you. However, if you are the nervous type and still find yourself struggling with social situations like these, here is some advice about active listening.

Active listening is where you listen for the sake of understanding, not for replying. Many people only stay silent in order to build a rebuttal, but if you are trying to get people to like who you are, it is best to understand what they are trying to say instead of spending energy and nerves scrambling for something to say in exchange. You want the others to feel safe around you and open up possibilities to meet up in the future. To be a good listener, do not judge. Let people talk and engage with them in their moments.

As you are listening, take note of how they sound. Do they sound happy? If they do, then perhaps what they are saying is going to lead to something funny. Do they sound disappointed? If they do, then perhaps you should offer some feedback by relating to a similar situation you once experienced. Do they sound irritated? If they do, then perhaps lending some advice to allow them to see a silver lining will help. Regardless of what you are listening to, always save what you want to say for last. To make sure they are done speaking, wait for them to fall silent. However, as someone meeting others for the first time, do not feel as though you can't say what is on your mind. Just remember, there are appropriate and inappropriate topics that will either have you liked by others or ignored.

As mentioned, body language accounts for fifty-five percent of effective communication. Body language is the first step in determining the direction of your conversation and even understanding if the other person is engaged or not. You should also be mindful of body language when speaking to others since you are part of the conversation and are trying to make an impression. A person's body language is based on their personality. For you, you want to use positive body language, not body language that tells others that you are not interested or that you are scared, fidgety, or anxious. The nonverbal movements and gestures convey messages of interest, enthusiasm, and positive reactions to what others are saying. If you want to make sure you aren't hurting your chances, try making a checklist of what to look out for.

Conversation Flow

There are few things more frustrating than not being able to get into a group or to make the person you want to talk ease up on you. People are often judgmental, and it is natural for people to feel distrust toward strangers. It is part of most people's upbringing to not talk to strangers. However, it may also be because they do not have encounters with a lot of people who they feel comfortable about themselves. Nobody wants to be put out of their comfort zone. However, with the right skills and know-how, you will have the ability to be placed out of the box.

You may sometimes feel that you are losing your

confidence whenever another person dismisses you. Do not feel dissuaded. Few people will allow you to join in abruptly if they are engaged in something important. You must learn to take things slowly. If you want to approach a group, make it a point that you show interest in the main speaker. Keep your distance but make sure that they see you. Your genuine interest will make them feel that it is necessary to invite you into their group.

Once you are in, make it a point that you listen to them first. Observe their body language and listen to how these people speak to one another. Without making a move, come up with a strategy. Pay attention to their body language; it will show you a lot about their personality. Wait for them to show you some signs that they believe that you are welcome in their group. Once they do, then you can start talking.

Make Them Lead the Talk

Here is a good strategy to remember, especially if you feel hesitant about talking to a group of strangers: these people like to talk. They like to talk about the topics they know about like their accomplishments and their dreams. They want to engage in conversations that make them feel good about themselves. That is what you should give them.

Here is the key to making conversations last the entire night: ask open-ended questions. Make sure that you just don't ask them where they work; ask them what they do for a living. Ask them about their family. Ask them about their upcoming vacations. Open-ended questions will keep them talking about themselves and will make them feel happy.

Use Enthusiasm

When you feel that they are talking about something that they are passionate about, make sure your emotion matches theirs. Use enthusiasm to reinforce their positive emotion. This strategy will make them feel that you understand their feelings and that you agree with their ideas.

Say Your Name and Ask for Theirs

A person who does not ask people their names is more likely not really interested in them. A person's name is the most important word for them. It is the first thing that they learned about themselves, and it is how they will know that you paid attention to all the things that they said and that you are looking forward to meeting them again. Make sure that you use the other person's name throughout the conversation.

Asking for another person's name is easy. However, it may be challenging for them to remember yours. Therefore, whenever you introduce yourself, say your name twice. For example, you can say, "I'm Bruce. Bruce Wayne" or "I'm Bruce Wayne, but you can call me Bruce."

If you want them to reach you after your initial engagement, you can give them your business card, but make sure that you ask for their card first. Asking for the other person's card is also a sure way for you to remember their name, and it will not be awkward to ask for their name again.

Should You Ask Them to Do Something for You?

This question is something that you would probably ask yourself if you are a salesperson or if you are in a business engagement and you need some people to listen to your pitch or ideas. It will be okay to do so after you have listened to them first. Alternatively, you can feel that it is okay to talk to people about what you do for a living once you can sense that there are a lot of things in common between you.

However, keep in mind that there is no one out there who will actually want to hear what you have to sell before you establish that you are their friend. So make sure that they feel at ease with you before you talk about whatever it is you are selling.

Principles for Success in Conversations

By following the tips outlined in this chapter, conversers will improve their small talk skills, have more meaningful conversations, and increase their likability.

Courage and Charisma

One of the greatest tips to understanding and learning about small talk and social interactions is how to share the information you possess. If you go through all the trouble of watching movies, reading books, and searching for all kinds of information to share but you are not particularly good at sharing the information, you might be disappointed with the results you get in the end.

People respond to your behavior and energy. If you seem dull and uninterested in the topic you talk about, then you will get little reaction. Do not perform some generic, robotic narration of information you have stored over a period of time. You need to be charismatic.

Natural charisma is a characteristic that only a few people possess, or so you may think. Anyone can be charismatic, and it only takes courage and motivation.

Courage is something you need to work on separately so as

to not have fear of talking in public or in having people judging you. Your fear will be lessened because you are sharing your personal interests and affiliations. You need to be confident in yourself and think of the information you are talking about like something that can change the world. It is that important.

No matter what you are talking about, your words are gold, and you need to treat them that way.

Apart from that, the motivation to talk about something and the passion that people easily fall in love with is something you need to produce yourself. You need to feel it, and it needs to be genuine. That will attract people to you.

The topic is irrelevant if you talk about it with passion like it is the most important thing in the world at that moment. You need to have some sort of measure of passion and importance according to the given topic so you won't seem strange and produce a negative reaction instead.

Ask Questions About the Other Person

Research shows that by being curious toward others and giving them an opportunity to share information about themselves, you can create positive feelings in them. To illustrate, according to a 2012 study by Diana I. Tamir and

Jason P. Mitchell titled "Disclosing Information about the Self Is Intrinsically Rewarding," sharing information about oneself correlates with increased activity in the area of the brain associated with pleasure. In fact, some people expressed a willingness to pay for such an opportunity. In other words, disclosing information about the self causes one to feel good. Therefore, you have the power to make others feel good by designing your conversations to include opportunities for your conversational partner to talk about him or herself. Be curious and ask questions.

Asking questions demonstrates curiosity and gives others an opportunity to share information about themselves. So an office employee might ask his new coworker, "Why did you apply for this job?" This question gives the new coworker an opportunity to share information about herself, such as her career goals, ambitions, and work philosophies.

In the early goings of a first date, one person might ask their date, "How long have you lived in this area?" This question opens up the door for the sharing of information such as past experiences in the area and fun things to do locally.

In a classroom, a student could ask a classmate, "Why did you choose this class?" This question invites the classmate to disclose things like educational goals, their major, and past experiences with the university or professors that they have had.

Of course, the office, a first date, and the classroom scenarios above only provide three examples of the limitless questions one can ask about another person. Those involved in real-life small talk should ask open-ended questions that are relevant to their immediate situation and invite self-disclosure. The next time you find yourself with time to spare, come up with three open-ended questions you can ask somebody in your setting.

Sharing information about the self feels good. After all, people devote about sixty percent of their conversations to talking about themselves, according to R. I. Dunbar, A. Marriott, and N. D. Duncan's 1997 study, "Human Conversational Behavior." If you can make your conversational partner feel good during a conversation with you, chances are they will like you and want to talk to you again in the future.

Ask Follow-Up Questions

Following up on open-ended questions with less abstract questions encourages more sharing and gives you and your conversation partner something more concrete to connect over. Try relating the follow-up question to the original question and answer. For example, if the office employee asks his new coworker, "Why did you apply for this job?" the new coworker might reply with something like "I wanted to be closer to my home, and I really like the company's environmental policy."

Given this reply, the office employee now has several pieces of information on which to build the conversation. The new coworker revealed that she used to commute farther than she does now, that she lives relatively close to the office, and that she cares about the environment. Here, the office employee can pick one of these pieces of information that interests him and ask a follow-up question about it. He might ask, "How long was your old commute?" Thus, the office employee demonstrates his curiosity, encourages sharing, and opens the door to the presence of even more potential topics of conversation. The next time you watch a talk show, pay attention to a guest's answer to one of the host's interview questions. Come up with a follow-up question you might ask the guest in a less time-constrained setting.

Share Information About Yourself

Much like getting others to share, sharing information about yourself is beneficial. Science further outlines the benefits of sharing information about yourself. Nancy L. Collins and Lynn Carol Miller reveal in their 1994 study,

"Self-Disclosure and Liking: A Meta-Analytic Review," that self-disclosure serves as a crucial part of long-term interpersonal relationships. The study found that self-disclosure makes people more likable and causes others to open up in return.

First, the researchers found that engaging in self-disclosure increases one's likability. In other words, the more information that one shares about oneself, the more others like them. On the other hand, those who share less information about themselves tend to have lower levels of likability. Refusal to share information about the self suggests that someone is hiding something or keeping a secret.

Second, engaging in self-disclosure can encourage your conversational partner to disclose information about themselves to you. Collins and Miller found that people tend to share more with people they like the most. Recall that sharing information about yourself can increase one's likability. By increasing your likability, you increase the likelihood that others will disclose to you. This brings out the pleasant feelings that you want your conversations to manifest in yourself and others.

Building off our example of the office employee and new coworker talking about commutes, we can examine how an opportunity for the office employee to self-disclose manifests in the conversation. The employee and his coworker's conversation might play out like this:

Office employee: "Hi! We haven't had a chance to talk much, but I was curious, what made you apply for this job?"

New coworker: "Well, the commute is a lot easier than my last job was. Plus, I'm a big fan of this company's environmental policy."

Office employee: "I see. How far did you commute for your last job?"

New coworker: "About ninety minutes each way."

(Here, the office employee has an opportunity to share his experiences with commuting.)

Office employee: "That's wild. I used to do work in the music industry, and it was the same thing every other weekend. I would travel to one city, often hours away, do my job, and then spend hours driving home the next day. What was the most exhausting commute you ever did?"

By sharing information with each other, the two conversers found themselves able to relate to each other's experiences surrounding the topic of commuting. From here, conversers should pay attention to their conversational partner's body language, as discussed earlier, for cues on how to carry on with the interaction.

Be Prepared

Sometimes participants may find that the conversation dies out before either party wants it to. In these cases, it is important for conversers to have new topics of discussion ready to bring up on demand. Prepare for lags in small talk by keeping up with current events and observing the setting.

Current events provide familiar topics of conversation. If you are informed on current events, you will likely find that they make for desirable topics of small talk. Current events are recent news stories involving well-known people, important places, and newsworthy occurrences. Examples of current events include celebrity gossip, political scandals, and natural disasters.

To revive a dying conversation, bring up a current event. You might introduce a current event with a question like "Did you hear about the fire in California?" This question invites your conversation partner to give their take on a widely discussed issue. News media often devote a lot of coverage to current events, so it is likely that others will have picked up a variety of viewpoints on these issues. Often, people are willing and eager to share their opinion on current events.

Alternatively, an observation or question about the setting can also bring a conversation back to life. In-person conversation partners share the same setting (such as two people who are in the same coffee shop). All parties to an in-person conversation have some relatable experience with the setting. For example, at a social gathering, ask your conversation partner to share their thoughts on the food with a simple, relatable question like "How do you like the food here?"

Also, consider sharing your thoughts first. You might begin with a statement like "I love the food here." This invites the other person to share their thoughts on the food as well, but you might have to ask them what their thoughts are. Right now, try coming up with three elements of your immediate setting that might make for topics of small talk.

When a conversation starts to fade, bring up a new topic as if it just entered your head. For example, revive a dying discourse with an inquiry like "Hey! Have you been to that new bar on the plaza?" Pay attention to how the other person responds. If they respond with enthusiasm and curiosity about the new topic, then continue the conversation with the willing individual. On the other hand, a short, one-word answer would suggest that they would rather let the conversation linger until it dies out. Either way, take your cue, and make a polite exit if their response calls for one.

Preparation can make all the difference in determining whether small talk dies out or flourishes. Be ready for lags in conversation. If you wish to continue small talk that you sense is fading, refer to a current event or an element of your setting. The next time you hear about a current event, think about how you might introduce it into a lulled conversation.

Demonstrate Vulnerability

In small doses, vulnerability can make one more likable. In the landscape of North America's hypercompetitive individualistic culture, people often fall into the trap of feeling as if they have to constantly one-up one another to the point of perceived invincibility. However, admitting to your shortcomings can actually make others perceive you as more trustworthy. Honesty demonstrates that you have nothing to hide.

Imagine that your boss has asked you to work on a new project that involves software you have never used before. You could easily tell your boss that it will not be a problem and you will complete the project. This approach is problematic because it requires that you spend time researching how to use the software on your own, which in turn causes you to turn in the project later than you would have if you knew how to use the software in the first place.

Instead, admit that you do not know how to use the software. Then your boss can work with you to compensate for your lack of familiarity with it. Your boss can give you more time to complete the project so you can learn how to use the software, give you an in-person software tutorial, or delegate the project to somebody more familiar with the software while you learn about it in the meantime. In any case, your boss will likely appreciate your honesty and will trust you more in the future. In return, you avoid the stress that comes along with having to compensate for a lie about your competency.

Give Compliments

When used appropriately, compliments can strengthen the bond between conversation partners. Research from the University of Tokyo, the Nagoya Institute of Technology, and the National Institute for Physiological Sciences suggest that compliments cause a neural reaction similar to the one that happens when we receive cash. In other words, compliments do the same thing to our brains that income does. It stands to reason then that compliments give people pleasurable emotions.

Compliments provide people with the recognition and acknowledgment that they crave. When complimenting others, make sure that the compliment comes from a place of genuineness. If you see your neighbor wearing a necklace that you like, tell them, "I like that necklace." Most likely, they will reply with gratitude. If you receive a compliment, smile, accept it, and express gratitude for it.

You can demonstrate the genuineness of your compliment by continuing to inquire about the object of your compliment. For example, follow up the compliment about your neighbor's necklace with a question like "What does the symbol on the pendant mean?" This follow-up question establishes that you are curious about the necklace that you claim to like. People tend to be curious about things that they like.

Compliments go a long way in establishing rapport between conversation partners. During small talk, offer a compliment on an element of your conversation partner that interests you, and then ask a question about it. Be warned, however: as stated earlier, experts recommend that in most situations, one should avoid making compliments regarding other people's body parts.

Ending Small Talk

Small talk eventually comes to an end. Conversers engaged

in small talk either move on to topics of more consequence or halt their interaction altogether. This section provides guidelines for ending a small talk on a positive note. When you feel that it is time to cut the interaction short, make a sincere positive remark, followed by either a recap of the conversation or a reason for abandoning the interaction.

Making a sincere positive remark begins the end of small talk. In most situations, a comment such as “Nice to meet you” will suffice. You may want your comment to remark on a specific aspect of your conversation. For example, after discussing a new project with your coworker, say something to the effect of “I’m happy we had the chance to talk. Our conversation gave me a lot of ideas for our upcoming project.” After a first date, one dater might signal the end of the interaction with a phrase like “I had so much fun this evening. The show was amazing.” Statements like these give the impression that the conversation is wrapping up. Right now, think back to the last conversation you had and come up with one nice thing you could say about that conversation.

After stating a sincere positive remark, summarize the interaction. To illustrate, imagine you have just made small talk with a classmate in the school’s hallway. To end the interaction, make a genuine, uplifting remark, such as “I had a great time talking with you,” followed by a summary of what was gained from your conversation. For example, "I'm glad to know I'm not the only one who feels that way about Professor Walt's class." The summary lets the other person know that you gained something from the interaction, retained information that they shared, and wish to complete the conversation. Right now, try to recall your last conversation and summarize it in one or two sentences.

Additionally, conversers have the option of following their summary with a plan for the future. This plan can take on many forms, including an invitation for future interaction, actions that one or both parties will take after they part ways, and vague implications of seeing each other again.

First, conversers can invite each other to interact again. Office coworkers might end with a plan to talk to each other at their next scheduled meeting. A friendly statement like "I will see you at the meeting tomorrow" serves as one such example of a plan. In a less formal situation, new acquaintances might say something like "I'm going to check out that new skate park tomorrow at three, if you want to meet me there." In any case, the plan should convey the idea that one conversation partner wants to continue to interact with the other. If somebody ends a conversation with a plan for future interaction, consider it an invitation to talk to him or her again.

Second, plans also take the form of future action to be taken. For example, you might say to your friend after a discussion about movies, "I will check out that alien movie you were telling me about." Future action also implies a desire to talk to the other person again. In this example, you and your friend will likely talk about the alien movie the next time you see them.

Third, vague implications of future interactions are another type of plan. As an example, you might end small talk with a phrase like "See you around!" or "I'll catch you later." Use vague statements like these when you would be happy to see the other person again, but you would also be okay with not coming into contact for a while.

Alternatively, a reason for ending the conversation can follow a sincere positive remark. By giving the person on the other end of your conversation a reason for leaving, you politely end the interaction. Reasons for leaving suggest that conversers do not necessarily want to end their conversation but instead have more pressing matters to take care of. A student making small talk with a classmate might follow up a nice comment with a reason for leaving and produce a conversation-ending statement like "It's been fun talking to you. Unfortunately, I have to head to the library to finish an assignment." The student gives his classmate a polite reason for ending the conversation. At this point, the student's classmate has the option to offer a plan for the future or not.

To end an instance of small talk, hint that you want to wrap things up by offering a positive statement. Next, give a summary, a summary and plan, or a reason for leaving. Try coming up with a reason for leaving your current setting that you might give someone else.

Chapter 6: How to Make a Great Impression

Ways to Make Other People Like You

It feels good to be liked. And being liked comes with benefits. People who like you will do more favors for you and will give you more ego-boosting compliments to build your confidence, which only makes you more attractive to others. Friends bring with them new connections and new opportunities in life, business, leisure—you name it. And above all, being popular makes other people assume that you are all right, so they will like you too. The more friends you have, the more friends you make, according to Dr. Robert Cialdini's social proof principle. Everyone wants to do what everyone else is doing, so if you are popular, you encourage others to like you just by being you.

But being liked is not just a natural talent that some people are born having. Yes, some people are born with the inherent skills of charisma. These skills are possible for anyone to learn, however. If you are not a naturally charismatic or radiant person, if you were never the popular kid in high school, and if you have trouble making friends, there is still plenty of hope for you.

Getting people to like you is as simple as appealing to human psychology. Through various scientific methods, you can make yourself more attractive to others and thus earn more friends and valuable connections. You just have to learn the tricks of the trade. Once you learn them, you will enjoy a vastly improved social life and many more social connections.

Cialdini's Principle of Social Proof

According to Cialdini's principle, if you appear to be a hot commodity, more people will want you. This principle works when picking up people at the bar or networking at a swanky event or just trying to make friends. If you show that someone likes you, then others think, "He must not be so bad. I can like him too."

If you show up to an event or party alone, you must rely on conversation skills to get others to like you. It can be hard to break the ice, particularly when everyone is in their own cliques and busy chatting with their own friends. It can also be tough if you are shy. It is far more helpful to show up with a buddy to prove that you are likable.

In the event that you have to be alone, try to find other people who are alone and bond with them. Once you have collected a little group of people to talk to, you appear more likable. Then others will gravitate toward you.

Another one of Cialdini's principles also applies to being well-liked. If you appear to be in short supply, the demand will increase for you. People operate on a scarcity mentality, where they have to have something that will soon run out. Appearing busy or unable to stay for long can make people feel more inclined to engage you in conversation.

Smile

Smiles are universal expressions of warmth, gratitude, and affection. All cultures engage in smiling. Smiling is important because it communicates a lot without words.

When you smile, you appear warm and nonthreatening, and thus you encourage others to approach you. And you appear like you are a confident, positive person who is not afraid to smile even when things are going wrong. Being the first to smile at someone is the same as being the first to approach them. In fact, a smile can be considered a type of approach or icebreaker.

A certain region of the brain called the orbitofrontal cortex activates when people see a smile. This area of the brain is responsible for seeing sensory rewards or pretty things. It is the part of the brain that goes, "Ooh, shiny!" A smile causes this part of the brain to light up on fMRIs, suggesting that people equate smiles with sensory rewards.

So when you smile at someone, you are lighting up his or her brain.

This study also suggests that people find smiling faces more attractive since their brains have the same reaction to smiling as they do to seeing beautiful faces. Even if you are not a supermodel, a smile can make you that much more lovely. People are more receptive to attractive faces. You will be liked more if you appear more attractive to others.

Smiling also causes some interesting chemistry to happen inside your own body. A smile will release neuropeptides, which fight stress, dopamine, serotonin, and norepinephrine. Thus, smiling helps you relax and restore your good mood. A heightened mood can also make you more likable and approachable because you are feeling good yourself. Just like how negativity is contagious, positivity is too.

One study shows that sixty percent of people can tell whether a smile is genuine or fake. That rate shoots up to sixty-six percent in a party atmosphere. Genuine smiles tend to get better reactions out of people than fake ones. So even if you don't feel like smiling much, think of something like cute puppies or your loved one, and smile like you mean it—it will make people like you so much more.

Show Genuine Interest in Other People

Being fake during a conversation is seldom wise. People tend to be poor judges of lies, but they can tell when something isn't right. So faking interest in a person is only going to lead to more awkward and uninteresting conversations.

Instead, show genuine interest. Ask people questions and try to learn more about them. Should a person bring up something you know nothing about, profess your ignorance and request for them to educate you. It will keep the conversation going.

Should a person really bore you, don't just feign interest. Shift the conversation onto more interesting grounds by asking a question or making a relevant comment. Keep things entertaining for everyone. It is an extremely valuable skill in a good conversationalist.

People love to feel important. If you show interest in them, then you give someone that sense of importance that releases all sorts of feel-good hormones in their brains.

Remember a Person's Name

What happens when you say someone's name? Certain centers of the brain activate in interesting ways. The medial frontal cortex gets particularly active. This activity indicates that when you hear your own name versus the names of others, you get excited and take special notice.

Hearing one's own name is an example of self-representational behavior. It triggers the medial frontal cortex because this is the part of the brain where a sense of self and personality are formed. When you see your reflection in a mirror and recognize yourself, your reaction is much different than when you see someone else in the mirror beside you. The reason for this reaction is because a different part of your brain activates when you see or hear anything pertaining to yourself.

Many teachers find it useful to memorize their students' names on the first day of class. Teachers who do have better bonds with their students and work better with the classroom as a whole because they make students feel good through self-representational models. They can lose that bond if they unintentionally forget a student's name.

Therefore, remembering a person's name is not just good manners. It is a scientific means by which you can get someone to like you. You make people happy and prove that you think them important when you bother to remember their names. Get their medial frontal cortexes happy by calling them by name!

Encourage Others to Talk About Themselves, and Listen Well

When people talk about themselves, try to listen well. People love to talk about themselves, so encourage it. The resulting dopamine flood will make them associate you with feeling good, and thus they will like you more.

Furthermore, you can encourage people by asking them questions about themselves. These questions should not be run-of-the-mill, yes-or-no questions. Ask involved questions like "How does that work?" or "How do you do that?" or "How does that make you feel?"

Speak to Others' Interests

Speaking to a person's interests holds their attention. No one likes to talk about something that is disinteresting to them. So you want to find topics that you both can enjoy discussing. Finding out what a person is into is helpful, but you should also find out what a person doesn't want to talk about as well.

People don't like to be rude (usually), so very few people will tell you outright when they are bored or offended. But the signs are clear. You just need to pay attention. People can communicate nonverbally through facial expressions, body language, and subconscious signals. A person will start looking around the room, eyeing the exit, fidgeting, or even giving fake smiles when he or she is anxious to leave a conversation that is no longer satisfying. When you spot these signs, it is a good cue to change the subject.

You may need to try many different subjects to find something to talk about, particularly with a shy or reticent person who lacks good conversation skills. Switching between topics can be jarring, but just keep trying until you find something that you can both relate to equally.

Make People Feel Important

Flattering someone in a genuine way is always a good way to score brownie points and get someone to like you. Paying attention is one way to make someone feel important, but there are other ways as well.

Maslow's hierarchy of needs is a social theory that points to how people need and want to feel. A person who is secure, happy, and satisfied is typically socially satisfied. Most people are insecure, however, and benefit from hearing that they are socially liked and needed. You want to appeal to that need for social satisfaction by letting someone know that he is important to others and serves a vital function in society.

Maslow's hierarchy of needs is commonly represented as a

pyramid. The very bottom layer consists of physical needs implicit to survival—food, shelter, water, sex. The next level up is the need for safety and security. People tend to worry most about these things when they are jeopardized, such as in a war-torn or poverty-stricken country.

The third level of the pyramid is love. People need to feel loved, at least by someone. Then there is self-esteem, where a person needs to feel good about himself and his accomplishments and needs confidence to approach life. At the very pinnacle of the pyramid is the need for self-actualization, which basically details the sense of accomplishing your purpose in life and somehow furthering the world with your personal contributions while using your abilities at their greatest capacity and unlocking all your potential.

When you let a person know how important he is, you satisfy the three upper levels of the pyramid or his need to be loved, to have self-esteem, and to fulfill his potential in life by actually mattering. You also let him know that his life's work is recognized and not wasted. Telling someone his accomplishments are important is the highest form of flattery. That is a big deal according to Abraham Maslow.

Basically, congratulate someone on his work or ask what he does for a living, and then comment about how important that job is. If a person is well known or at least known by you, be sure to say that so that you appear like a big fan.

Wear Red

This weird little tip works. The human brain is wired to respond well to red. Wearing red, even just in your hat or tie, can make others like you. It makes others assume you are a warm, trustworthy, and relatable person.

In a study, men approached women wearing red lipstick the most often. People wearing red were also ranked "more attractive." And women tend to view men wearing red or with red hair as more approachable and more suitable for romantic pursuits. The conclusion is that while red can be the color of pain and danger, it is also somehow an attractive, warm, and even seductive color. People are drawn to red. They will certainly notice you if you wear it.

Try red lipstick or a red dress as a woman, or a red tie or shirt as a man. Consider a red coat or hat in winter months and a red umbrella on rainy days. In little ways, up the amount of red you wear to become more likable.

Chapter 7: How to Connect and Make Someone Feel Connected with You

Personal relationships are what make life worth living. Even if you consider yourself an introvert, you need human interaction to survive in this world.

As humans, we are hardwired to seek out relationships and create alliances with one another. Our ability to communicate and empathize with each other is what sets us apart and makes us human beings. Although it is innate in every single one of us to want to connect with other people, most of the time, it is difficult to make those connections. Sure, some people may be better at building rapport than others, but that doesn't mean that you should stop trying.

The bonds that we build are not only crucial in getting ahead in our careers, they are also essential in building happy and satisfied lives. Human connection is not only good for our emotional state but can also boost our physical health.

So what does it really mean to connect with people, and how can you tell if you are actually connecting with someone?

More than just engaging in conversation about shared interests, real connection happens when you open yourself up to be vulnerable to another person, and they also feel the same toward you. Real connection is when you feel a sense of goodwill toward another, marked by some degree of empathy or compassion. It is not just merely engaging someone and inviting them into a conversation; it is about building rapport with someone with the hope that it could lead to a deeper understanding of each other.

Developing a connection with someone, especially with a total stranger, can be tricky. Sometimes you think you can connect with others by being smart, interesting, or funny; but if you are always relying on other people's reactions before you act, then that is not really connecting. Check your heart because you might just be fueling your need to be accepted or vying for attention. If you have to work too hard at it, then it is not really a connection. Here are the five signs that you are truly connecting with someone.

Five Telltale Signs You Are Connecting with Someone

1. You Are Completely Present in the Moment

It is impossible to develop a real connection with someone if you are preoccupied with past or future worries. Being distracted by other things robs you of the opportunity to share an experience with someone else. So if you find yourself in the present moment with someone; it is a sign that you are connecting.

2. You Are Not Afraid to Be Yourself

Many people have this incorrect notion that in order to be liked by someone, they need to hide their true selves. The thing is, real human connections can only flourish with honesty. So if you are not afraid to show who you really are to another person, it means that you are allowing that person to know the real you.

3. You are Letting Down Your Guard

Another sign that you are connecting with someone is that you are slowly letting down your guard. Opening up to someone takes significant courage, so sharing a side of you that you wouldn't normally share is a sign that you are willing to be vulnerable to develop a connection. Incidentally, sharing your moment of weakness with another person is a powerful way to build a connection with them.

4. You Feel a Sense of Compassion toward the Other Person

Here is the hard truth. You wouldn't care about another person if you didn't share a connection. Being indifferent or judgmental toward someone else is a sign that you don't share any bond with the person. Since human bond is strengthened with kindness, feeling compassion toward someone else is a sign that you have a connection.

5. You Feel You Can Trust the Other Person

You cannot build a relationship without trust, so if you feel like you can trust another person, that is a good sign that there is a real connection. To trust someone is probably one of the hardest things to do in the world because it is more common to be suspicious of other people. So if you feel like trust can exist between you and another person, it means you are willing to build something deeper with them.

Have you ever met someone with whom you felt an instant connection even though you have just met? We all have. Now try to think of what set that person apart from everyone else. What was it that made you comfortable? Maybe it was the warm feeling that you got when you were talking with the person. Or it could also be because that person had a smile that made you feel at ease. Whatever it was that drew you to the person, you can replicate it yourself to create a connection with someone else. At the end of the day, the principles of building human connection remain the same.

The Ten Principles of Deeper Human Connection

1. Give Your Full Attention

The first principle of creating a connection with someone is to pay attention. When another person is talking to you, it is crucial that you focus not just on the words they say but on the message that they are trying to convey. You can learn a lot about a person by paying attention to their words and actions.

But because we live in a world that is filled with distractions, giving your full attention to someone can be a bit of a challenge. Checking your phone for new messages, for example, or failing to make eye contact with the person you are talking to can seem dismissive or rude. If you want to make a connection with someone, make that person your priority—even for just the moment.

2. Make Your Best First Impression

It may be hard to accept, but people will judge you based on their first impression of you. They won't just notice the words you say but also the way you carry yourself and even the facial expressions that you make. If you are not aware of your body language, you could end up misunderstood or giving them a bad first impression.

You don't have to pretend to be someone you are not to make a good impression. You just have to present the best version of yourself. Now is the perfect time to check yourself for any personal quirks and habits that are making you seem less approachable.

3. Remember Names

While it is true that there are only a few people who can put names to faces, putting effort into remembering the names of people you have just met is one of the best ways to connect with someone. Remembering someone's name will not only make them feel welcome but will also make them feel a bond with you.

So how do you remember the names of people you have just met? One trick is to include their name into the conversation as many times as you can. But of course, try to make it sound natural so it doesn't seem like you are a broken record. You can also ask people about their hobbies and pastimes so that you can find something unique about them that will help you remember who they are.

4. Tell Your Story

Another effective way to get people to connect with you is

to tell a memorable story about yourself. Your story or narrative should give people a deeper insight into who you really are and what you stand for. Be ready to share some of your experiences, life goals, and desires with others.

Telling an interesting story is far more engaging than if you were to tell someone you have just met hard facts about yourself. Stories can capture people's attention, while facts are just pieces of information that can easily be forgotten. By telling your story, people won't just get a closer look into your thoughts and beliefs, they will also feel more comfortable sharing their own stories with you.

5. Offer Something of Value

You can also create a connection by offering something of value to the other person. By helping out and being of service to others, you are making yourself irresistible to other people. Why? Because even though we don't like to admit it, people are naturally drawn to those who have something that they want or need.

Offering something of value does not mean that you should start giving things away. Think of ways that you can help others, even in small ways. Maybe it is sending over a link to a TED talk on a topic that they are passionate about or giving them leads to a job or project that you think they would be perfect for. By wanting the best for others, you are making it easier for a connection to develop naturally.

6. Come Prepared

Social settings can be quite stressful because most of the time you won't really know what to expect. If the thought of striking up a conversation with strangers is enough to make your palms sweat, then you should probably do some research in advance. Doing a little groundwork before you get yourself out there will not only alleviate stress, but it will also make it easier for you to focus on making a connection with people you are going to meet.

Doing prep work, like coming up with a list of thought-provoking questions, will help you feel more relaxed and confident as you talk to new people. Reading up on current events is also a good way to have a few conversation starters up your sleeve. But make sure that your questions or topics are not too invasive or personal, as you do not want to cause offense to anyone.

7. Spark Interest

There are times when you don't really need to try too hard to make a connection. Sometimes all it takes is your unique sense of fashion or your quirky sense of humor. Is there something about you that naturally just sparks interest in strangers? Whatever it is, so long as it is not going against normal conventions or causing offense to anyone, by all means, flaunt it. Think of it as your very own conversation starter.

Whether it is your fondness for vintage watches or a signature hair color, these unique details can make you seem more approachable to people, especially to those who have the same interests as you. It is your chance to show off a little flair and stand out from the crowd.

8. Show Your True Self

The more genuine you are, the more people will want to get to know you, so do not be afraid to wear your heart on your sleeve. Do not be afraid to share your ideas, beliefs, and goals with others because once you start talking, they will be more comfortable sharing more information about themselves.

In showing your true self, just remember not to monopolize the conversation. Always give the other person space to share their own ideas, beliefs, and goals. Be careful not to lecture others or convert them to your cause. The goal here is to share what you are passionate about to other people so that they will be more open to sharing their own passions. This sharing could lead to deeper conversations or even friendly debates.

9. Listen and Learn

No one likes a know-it-all, so make sure that you take the opportunity to listen and learn from others. It is always a good idea to share the stage with someone else instead of showing off or one-upping the other person.

By listening to what other people have to say and learning from their experiences, you are breaking down the walls between you. You are not just going to see a different point of view, you are also giving the other person the opportunity to offer something of value to you.

10. Be Human

Showing empathy, kindness, and gratitude will always be the best way to make a connection, so remember to be human when interacting with people. Choose to be courteous every chance you get, and if there is something that another person has given or taught you, make it your cardinal rule to express your gratitude. Sometimes a simple thank you is enough to start a connection.

Being positive and uplifting will help you build relationships wherever you go. Aim to make friends and not just acquaintances because, at the end of the day, that is all there is to connecting with people. You don't need to overthink it because people have the natural tendency to bond together when they find people with whom they are comfortable.

But what if you are one of those people who finds it hard connecting with others? What if for some reason or another, you get nervous about interacting with other people? What do you do then?

Chapter 8: How to Tell a Great Story Without Being Boring

Principles of a Good Storyteller

There are two kinds of conversations—one is about a topic that means something and has a measure of substance, and the other is exploratory conversation. In the course of a new meeting, a session can be one or the other, or it can span across both.

For new acquaintances, a conversation that spans across both is an indication that there is substantive chemistry or personal chemistry between the participants. For those who do not arrive at this stage during every meeting, there isn't any cause to be concerned. It does not mean one is a failed effort and the other is a successful one.

Most first-time conversations end at the exploratory stage. The exploratory stage is the period of the conversation where you and your conversation partner are looking for common ground. He is looking for the boundaries of the budding relationship and trying to find where you fit in his landscape, while you are doing the same. The exploratory conversation also gives rise to an opportunity to assess the person's vibe.

We often mistake the value of giving out positive vibes and miss the opportunity to make an impression. Vibes do a lot to cement the connection and act as a bridge over which your words and content traverse. Without the vibe, every word and gesture you manufacture is going to labor its way across to the other side.

Here are ten things you need to keep at the back of your mind when you start practicing the art of conversation and it comes to keeping the conversation interesting.

1. Introduction

Keep the introduction short and sweet. Think up ways that allow people to remember your name. Even if you have a name that is easy to remember, do not be fooled; you still want the person to attach your name to your face. So whether you have a unique name that is hard to remember or an easy name that is common, you need to spend some time on your own, thinking of an opening line so that people will remember your name. For instance, if your name is Joe, you could tell them that your friends used to call you Mojo when you were younger but you don't go by that anymore. The psychology behind this is that you personalize your name with a unique story. It also helps to break the ice.

Short, sweet, and smooth—the triple *S* of introductions. In an introduction, you are aiming for the person to remember your name and for you to get their full name. Don't get too deep too quickly. The questions you ask will set the tone of the conversation.

If you are a man talking to a woman, asking if she is married in the first few minutes of the introduction may seem like it is getting to the point, but it is also communicating to the person that you are looking for a date even if you are not. Instead, keep the introduction to the point where you know what to call him or her and launch from there.

2. Interest

Show genuine interest in the person with whom you are talking. Showing genuine interest keeps the person engaged longer. You show interest by asking nonintrusive questions. Each question you pose that is easy to answer builds their confidence and puts them in the habit of answering you. But the benefit is that you don't have to do the talking to keep the conversation going. All you have to do is listen and ask follow-up questions. Again, make sure they are not intrusive.

The questions can get more personal as you start to observe them, lowering their guard.

3. Be Nonjudgmental

Never be judgmental. Whatever they tell you, never judge. You are not there to preach. You are not there to punish or to convince the world of your brand of morals. You are there to make an acquaintance and to keep the conversation going so that you find out more about them.

4. Follow Up

Base your questions on what the person just told you. Ask follow-up questions.

5. Watch for Feedback

Remember that you are part of a live conversation. Don't just walk on stage and spill a whole bunch of canned questions. Keep it interactive. Watch for signs and gestures; look at expressions. Gage how well they are progressing in the conversation.

These first five steps are concerned with the strategy of conversation from an introductory perspective. The second set of steps will look at it from a qualitative perspective.

6. Prompt questions

Prompting your counterpart to ask you questions so that you have the opportunity of answering is a good way to keep the conversation flowing. Learn how to insert cliffhangers. That way, you get them interested enough to ask questions. If you listen carefully to what your counterpart has to say, using what they have said in the past, you can draw inferences and draw similarities and tell them that you have had a similar experience. This statement should prompt them to ask you questions, which then gives you the opportunity to respond. If they run out of questions and you want to continue the conversation, then it is your turn to ask questions again.

Remember, keeping a conversation alive does not mean that you do all the talking. You should be more silent than conversant, but your body language should be in total focus to your current approach.

7. Time Spent

Get an idea of the time that you should spend on each conversation. If you are at a function and there are numerous people you want to meet, it is also logical to assume that the other person also wants to meet many people. So don't monopolize the conversation for too long. Find an opportunity to get contact information, and then move on.

8. Speak Calmly

The common mistake among potential conversationalists

is that they can't modulate their voices to within the comfortable range. Most people think that they can't control their voice beyond their normal volume. That is not entirely true. If you can't get a voice coach, you can find interesting tips online to change the timbre and register of your voice. It is a fact that men with lower voices seem to score better at being trustworthy. And you can train yourself to speak with a lower voice. Just keep practicing, and eventually it will be the voice you use. More important than changing your register is the fact that you have to speak clearly. Clarity and enunciation allow the listener to easily understand your point. If they don't understand, they can't be interested.

9. Stay Positive

The anchor in any conversation is a positive, can-do tone and enthusiasm. You want to spread the cheer and pick up people's moods, not pile them with doom and gloom. Those kinds of conversations begin with a lot of theatrical value but fizzle out in short order. These kinds of conversations do not have any kind of personal longevity. No one is going to look forward to when they can meet up with you. Negativity does not work in the long run.

10. Do Not Over Gesticulate

A certain amount of body movement and hand gestures is

a great way to animate your subject matter and keep your counterpart awake and following. But after a while, those movements can add up and become excessive. They can be distracting to some people, they can have a physical effect on others, and to some sensitive people, they can even trigger nausea. Stand firm and wear a smile—that is all that is necessary.

These ten items are a great place for you to start. But as always, you must know that there is no hard and fast rule to super conversations or super conversationalists. You have to start somewhere, and these ten steps can help you to do that. This book gives you the initial push in the right direction, but you have to practice, make mistakes, reevaluate, and keep going if you want to become a strong conversationalist.

How to Keep the Other Person Engaged and Listening

Conversations do not get interesting by chance. When a person gets engaged in a conversation, they do so for selfish reasons, just like you. If you are doing it for selfish reasons and they are doing it for selfish reasons, then it stands to reason that there is going to be a mutually beneficial outcome.

In a conversation, the typical selfish reason why people converse is to satisfy their need for social engagement. They want to build their contact base with a person or a group who has something to offer, and they want to learn something that will have material benefits at some point in the future. There is always an angle.

You need this underlying knowledge to keep it interesting. While you don't want to drop names more than just once or twice in one evening (as name-dropping can be a hinderance to small talk), who you know is a great way to keep a conversation alive and create a steep hill of authority. You will gain authority by association. Say, for instance, you have some form of connection to the White House, perhaps for some work you do. If you were to casually mention that you had been to the White House and that the president dropped in on a meeting you were attending, that little morsel of information just turned the entire conversation around and made it interesting.

You also want to be able to know your material. If you are able to come up with facts that are true and you show expert handling of those facts, that makes the conversation interesting. At the same time, reserve your judgment about something and stay positive. For instance, if you are having a conversation about gun control, you should stake your position and not be combative about it. You must be able to quote facts and assumptions in making your case. But while you are doing it, stay compassionate to your opponent's position.

It is worthwhile to remember that a conversation is not a debate. Do not get drawn into one. A conversation is not hostile. Keeping it interesting is about having a mutually satisfying session.

Another dimension from which you should launch off is that you have zero expectations of what the other person is going to do or how they will respond. You can have a goal, but do not cultivate an expectation. Having expectations only makes the conversation rigid and leads to possible frustration.

Always include anecdotal information. It is always nice to have something entertaining to deliver the point rather than just having the statistics and data constantly thrown at you. Keep the information functional rather than theoretical.

One other element that you can use to keep things interesting is if you understand the other person's trigger points. You will be able to figure these out if you have been paying attention from the beginning. If you see interest waning, just switch to one of the topics that you know will surely be popular with your counterpart.

Finally, keep it interesting by following the agenda of the session. If you are meeting for a stated reason, fulfill that reason. Do not go off topic.

Chapter 9: What to Do When You Find Yourself in a Group Conversation

Good social skills hinge on being able to relate and talk to others in a normal fashion. They can also mean the difference between superfluous small talk and warm, meaningful connections. If you want more people to like you, you must learn how to talk to people in a likable way.

The main component to a great conversation is empathetic listening. You may be a great listener, but how do you show it? The answer is simply by being obvious about your empathetic listening. That way, you will excite the other person, proving that you care about what he or she has to say. However, to be an empathetic listener, you must prove that you are listening.

While someone talks, look directly at the person and/or nod and interject with the occasional affirmative motion. When the person pauses, you may mention something directly related to what he or she is saying. Conversely, changing the subject, interrupting, staring into space, and appearing impatient for your turn to talk are all good ways to alienate the talker and ruin the conversation. You want to appear interested by making eye contact and by practicing reflective listening.

Reflective listening refers to the method of repeating what someone says, showing them that you really did hear what they just said. You may repeat things verbatim, or you may rephrase them. Similarly, you may also come back with a reply that proves you were paying attention and are absorbing what the person is saying.

There are different kinds of conversationalists. For example, some just talk forever, never paying attention to social cues, causing them to bore and drive other people away. Then there are wallflowers, who don't talk to anyone as they carefully observe their surroundings. Finally, there are confident interactors, who enjoy talking to others and listening to their stories with genuine interest. You can see which of the three is the most likable. You want to aim for confident interaction at all times when relating to others.

If you are a shy person, injecting yourself into a conversation can pose a challenge. You may feel inclined to just sit back and listen. While listening is great (because it is the most important foundation of good conversation), you lack the other component—talking about yourself. You must be willing to talk as well as listen if you want your conversations to go anywhere. Otherwise, you will bore people and come across as a silent wallflower with nothing to add to the conversation. If this happens, the only people who will talk to you will be the blowhards who talk incessantly and don't know when to shut up. You can avoid these problems by having confident interactions.

The key here is to actually talk to the person with whom you are conversing. A conversation goes two ways, and you must do your part to keep it going. On top of listening, you should start speaking. Do not just interrupt by blurting out whatever comes to mind or by attempting to change the subject constantly. It is best to actually find relevant topics to bring up.

A relevant topic may be based on what the other person starts talking about. If you want to give the other person control of the conversation, then you can just go along with what he or she talks about. This strategy is a good way to start practicing conversation with people if you are shy.

However, you can also take charge of conversations and propose your own topics. Wait for the other person to stop talking, and then bring up a new topic. Possibly find topics that are somehow related to the original one proposed by the other person so that there is a logical flow to the conversation.

Starting a conversation first gives you more control of the interaction and allows you to make a solid impression. You can start talking to someone and find ways to relate. Tip: keep mentioning topics until you find one that takes off.

The most relevant topic is one that can bond you and your conversation partner. Finding topics that actually interest both of you is a good way to pass the time without causing boredom or frustration. You will want to find things with which you can relate to your conversation partner, and the more you find in common, the more you will like each other. Briefly introduce yourself and talk about what you enjoy and see if your conversation partner resonates with anything you say.

Asking questions that lead to a person talking about themselves is another way to start a good conversation. Keep the focus on your conversation partner by asking them questions about themselves. Ask what they like and for more details about their job. Then if they mention any topic, you should ask them to expand on it. People love to talk about themselves, so this questioning can really encourage a person to open up and like you.

Similarly, you may inadvertently repel conversation and relationships with negativity. For instance, if someone mentions fly-fishing and you say, “I hate fly-fishing,” you are creating a negative factor, which can halt the bonding experience. It is far better to stay positive and say something like “I have never tried fly-fishing” or “I’m not much of a fishing person, to be honest, but I do love being outdoors.” Both examples dangle the possibility of still finding something in common in front of your conversation partner, even if you don’t enjoy the particular hobby of fly-fishing.

It has been found that people who share more and act more intimate or familiar right away tend to make a better impression and make more friends. Therefore, you can actually enjoy more conversational success by acting more familiar with people you have just met. This advice applies to the warmth factor mentioned earlier. You may feel that it is wrong and that asking personal questions is rude, but people will actually open up to you more if you do.

This idea was proven by an interesting experiment where people were divided into two groups and members were assigned random partners. In one group, the pairs were told to exchange small talk; the other group was told to ask very personal questions from a list. All participants rated how much they liked one another before the experiment and after. The members of the group who exchanged personal questions liked one another the most at the study’s end because they were actually able to form a bond and get to know one another.

Naturally, this study does not mean that you should ask offensive or upsetting questions, nor will you want to ask someone about their religious or political affiliations, as these types of questions can invite controversy and unpleasantness. Instead, ask personal questions that people might enjoy answering. Your goal is to get someone to divulge information to you so that you can find common ground over which to bond.

You might start conversations with refreshing personal questions that most people don't ask. For example, you might ask someone what they would do if they were to find out that they have one day left to live, or what their dream job was when they were still a kid. You might also consider asking someone about the best book they ever read or the most vivid dream they ever had. Because questions are not your typical, run-of-the-mill conversation starters, they will intrigue and interest your conversation partner and make for quite a dynamic conversation.

Another key to good conversation is to pay careful attention to the ebb and flow of the conversation. If a person starts to withdraw or look bored, don't take it personally. Instead, take it as a sign that you should change the subject. Similarly, if a person starts to get upset, you should definitely change the subject. Consider how to soothe and reassure a person who is not enjoying the topic. Be sure to acknowledge a person's feelings by saying "I can see this is really important to you" or "I can see that this upsets you a lot." This kind of emotional recognition makes a person feel validated. Validation is key to being liked.

You are not responsible for how someone feels, but if you want to have a good conversation, you should try to keep things pleasant and light. No one really wants to talk about heavy topics, especially if they don't know you well.

Confident interaction involves showing that you are invested and interested. You must listen, and you must speak. Maintaining the flow of conversation by going back and forth on relevant topics is the basis of the social skill of good conversation.

Conclusion

You now have everything you need and more to start improving your conversation skills and become better at small talk. It may take time and effort, but if you keep practicing, eventually you will get there. It is not a skill or technique you need to be born with; it is not an exceptional talent you need to possess to become good. Learning great conversation skills is something that everyone can do.

All it takes is practice. Start practicing the techniques you have learned in this book and putting them into practice at every opportunity you get. The more you practice, the better you will become, and one day you will master the art of small talk. As your conversation skills start to improve, you will notice that your confidence in conversing with people also enhances in tandem. With enough practice, you will have the ability to hold a conversation with anyone, even complete strangers.

Editor's Critique:

Overall, this book is informative and inspirational. It provides a wealth of information about the art of conversations, and it gives practical advice and suggestions